THE CROSS
OF HOPE

The Cross of Hope
Words of encouragement for the imperfect disciple

Tony Philpot

Kevin Mayhew

First published in 1996 by
KEVIN MAYHEW LTD
Rattlesden
Bury St Edmunds
Suffolk IP30 0SZ

© 1996 Kevin Mayhew Ltd

The right of Tony Philpot to be identified as the author
of this work has been asserted by him in accordance with
the Copyright, Designs and Patents Act 1988.

All rights reserved. No part of this publication may be
reproduced, stored in a retrieval system, or transmitted,
in any form or by any means, electronic, mechanical,
photocopying, recording or otherwise, without the
prior written permission of the publisher.

0 1 2 3 4 5 6 7 8 9

Scripture quotations are from the New Revised Standard Version
of the Bible, copyright 1989 by the Division of Christian Education
of the National Council of the Churches of Christ in the USA.
Used by permission.

ISBN 0 86209 904 8
Catalogue No 1500075

Front cover: *A Flowery Glade* by Alfred Parsons (1847-1920).
Reproduced by courtesy of Mr Fulda,
Fine Art Photographic Library, London.

Cover design by Veronica Ward and Graham Johnstone

Typesetting by Vicky Brown
Printed and bound in Great Britain

Contents

Preface	7
In the Heart of God *John 1:1-18*	9
Justified by His Blood *Romans 5:1-11*	17
Time for Tenderness *Matthew 27:27-50*	25
Suffering Servant *2 Corinthians 1:3-11*	35
Good News to the Poor *Luke 11:37-54*	45
Awake, Sleeper *Romans 8:28-39*	55

Preface

Things get crystallised in your mind. If I say to you, 'Remembrance Sunday', or 'school dinners', or 'airport lounges' or 'going to the dentist', I trigger off a familiar train of memories, a succession of images. It is as if we think in clichés. We're like slide projectors. Click, click, click, the pictures pass before our eyes.

'Calvary' is one of these triggers. We each have our series of snapshot pictures of Calvary. But snapshots don't tell the whole truth, only an aspect of it, only one perspective of it. This little book is an attempt to make our reflection on the dying and rising of Christ a fraction richer and deeper, perhaps to provide some more images.

The whole truth isn't told here, either. Nothing like. The death and resurrection of Jesus is a mystery, meaning a reality which God gradually unfolds and reveals to us. We approach it with extreme reverence and awe, like Moses taking his shoes off before the burning bush. Every time I reflect on Calvary and Easter there is more to discover, more to appreciate. No book, however long, can say adequately what needs to be said.

Prayer is another mystery. What happens to a believer when he rests his or her mind and heart on the living God? People have tried to describe it, but it remains intensely personal, and often beyond words. It is the supreme Christian experience. The same experience tells us that it may take a word from outside ourselves, rather like the ignition in a car, to spark us into prayer. Scripture, clearly, is the best ignition. But if any of the reflections which follow do this for the reader, they will have served their purpose.

TONY PHILPOT

In the Heart of God

John 1:1-18

In the beginning was the Word, and the Word was with God, and the Word was God. He was in the beginning with God. All things came into being through him, and without him not one thing came into being. What has come into being in him was life, and the life was the light of all people. The light shines in the darkness, and the darkness did not overcome it.

There was a man sent from God, whose name was John. He came as a witness to testify to the light, so that all might believe through him. He himself was not the light, but came to testify to the light. The true light, which enlightens everyone, was coming into the world.

He was in the world, and the world came into being through him; yet the world did not know him. He came to what was his own, and his own people did not accept him. But to all who received him, who believed in his name, he gave power to become children of God, who were born, not of blood or of the will of the flesh or of the will of man, but of God.

And the Word became flesh and lived among us, and we have seen his glory, the glory as of a father's only son, full of grace and truth. (John testified to him and cried out, 'This was he of whom I said, "He who comes after me ranks ahead of me because he was before me."') From his fullness we have all received, grace upon grace. The law indeed was given through Moses; grace and truth came through Jesus Christ. No one has ever seen God. It is God the only Son, who is close to the Father's heart, who has made him known.

Matthew, Mark and Luke begin their Gospels on the soil, and among the people, of the Holy Land. Matthew starts with a family tree; Mark with a Jewish preacher; Luke with a childless Judaean couple. There is something reassuring and familiar about all this. It's as though they were coming to meet us on our own ground, with ordinary, human beginnings to their story.

But John begins his Gospel outside time. He begins it in the mind and heart of God, who was there before there was any world, or any time. You get the feeling, after the other three Gospels, that the centre of gravity suddenly shifts. Where, after all, he is asking, is reality rooted? In the experience of us, of men and women? Or – much more difficult for us to grasp – in the being of God himself, in his will and in his intention?

Where does our story start, the story of the Passion? I am quite convinced that it starts in the unfathomable mercy of God. God made this material universe of ours, one way or another, out of nothing (let's not concern ourselves with the details, whether it was a Big Bang or not . . . in the end, it makes little difference). And then God made us human beings (let's not concern ourselves with the details, whether it was a slow process or a quick one . . . in the end, it makes little difference). The main thing is that he made us, and gave us extraordinary gifts of spirit and self-determination, so that we could be, quite consciously, the stewards of his creation; so that we could detect the spark of immortality he had planted in us. And yet, in the very act of creating, he already knew – he must have known – what ambiguous creatures we would be and are. He knew our capacity for waywardness as well as our capacity for love. And already, all that time ago, he was planning our rescue. That is the incredible thing.

This is a far cry, isn't it, from the blood and sweat of Calvary; from the panic of Peter, and the cynicism of Pilate, and the kangaroo courts, and the midday heat and the final prayer of the Good Thief? And yet none of this, in all its detail, none of those things we recall with reverence now, could have taken place without that decision in principle which the Father took at the beginning of time; really outside time.

Here, then, is the unanswerable question. Why has God this clinging affection for our human race, this unquenchable desire and determination to bring it home to himself? It's a desire which causes God (who is immortal and invisible) to get entangled, himself, in our affairs; to take our flesh, to suffer our condition, to die our death. It seems out of all proportion, doesn't it? Christianity is founded on a breach in the logic of things. How right God is to say, 'My thoughts are not your thoughts, nor are your ways my ways'.

I don't understand it because I am not God: I can't see with his eyes or love with his heart. I can only say this: that it seems to me as though, having made us in his own image and likeness – having made us basically spiritual, in other words – he has invested so much in us that he cannot afford to let us go. We are now worth saving at any price – even the price of his Son. And so, 'the Word became flesh, and lived among us'.

St John's perspective is right: he sees the story of Christ's passion and death from God's point of view. 'The true light, which enlightens everyone, was coming into the world. He was in the world, and the world came into being through him; yet the world did not know him.'

Against this background – that of the eternal plan of God – the story of our Lord's passion and death has a really awesome quality. If it were a Greek tragedy you were reading, and not the Gospel of Jesus Christ, it would make you hold your breath. Surely, now, after Good Friday, you would say, God must finally obliterate humanity. The only question is, when will he do it? When will Nemesis strike? Because we have taken his divine and sinless Son, his Messenger, and rejected him and mocked him, abused and tortured him, priced him at 30 silver pieces and killed him. 'He came to what was his own, and his own people did not accept him.'

I don't know what you can say about a humanity like this. That it's incurably vicious? That it's fatally accident-prone? Because we couldn't have got it more wrong. This is a disaster of cosmic proportions. The crucifixion is like the distillation of all the blindness, foolishness, narrow-mindedness, stubbornness and cruelty: all the dark underside of the human character is here to see.

It is at this point that the Father shows us how different he is from us: 'For my thoughts are not your thoughts, nor are your ways my ways.' Thank God for that. Because instead of bringing down on humanity the hammer of annihilation, which is what you would have done or I would have done, God takes the cosmic disaster and turns it into a cosmic victory.

For in God's book, you win not by muscle but by love. The love of Christ proves stronger than anything that can be done to him. You have to match on the one hand the *realpolitik* of Annas and Caiaphas, the supercilious might of Rome and Pilate's tribunal, the sadistic cruelty of the mercenary soldiers . . . against on the other hand Christ's heroism, integrity, self-sacrifice, enduring forgiveness, implicit trust in his Father. Our world says, regretfully, that the nails and the spear win, the meek and innocent lose. But God replies, 'You're wrong. God's weakness is stronger than human strength. My power is made perfect in weakness.' And so Good Friday is followed by Easter Sunday, the crucifixion by the resurrection.

That's why the cross becomes our flag, our standard. We place it on the rooftree of our churches, we install it at the top of mountains; we put it on walls and on desks; we incorporate it in a hundred different logos and emblems and badges, so that, to use an Old Testament expression, it is constantly before our eyes. We are the people who do not believe that might is right. We are the people, to quote St Paul, who believe that God's strength is made perfect in our weakness. You can imagine nothing weaker than Jesus – rejected by the people, sentenced by the occupying power, scourged and crucified. Yet out of this dreadful mess comes the resurrection.

And out of it, too, comes a message from the Father to us. Two messages, in fact. One is, 'You are precious in my eyes. When you look round at the human race, and the pits it digs for itself, and the black passages in its history, you may be tempted to say, "We are an unlovable lot". It isn't so. In spite of everything, I love you. So, lift up your heads, claim your dignity – and treat one another with that same dignity.' And the other is, 'Remember where the moral victory lies: not with the bully-boy, the manipulator and the trickster; but with the man or woman of integrity'. And the moral victory is the real victory.

JUSTIFIED BY HIS BLOOD
Romans 5:1-11

Therefore, since we are justified by faith, we have peace with God through our Lord Jesus Christ, through whom we have obtained access to this grace in which we stand; and we boast in our hope of sharing the glory of God. And not only that, but we also boast in our sufferings, knowing that suffering produces endurance, and endurance produces character, and character produces hope, and hope does not disappoint us, because God's love has been poured into our hearts through the Holy Spirit that has been given to us.

For while we were still weak, at the right time Christ died for the ungodly. Indeed, rarely will anyone die for a righteous person – though perhaps for a good person someone might actually dare to die. But God proves his love for us in that while we still were sinners Christ died for us. Much more surely then, now that we have been justified by his blood, will we be saved through him from the wrath of God. For if while we were enemies we were reconciled to God through the death of his Son, much more surely, having been reconciled, will we be saved by his life. But more than that, we even boast in God through our Lord Jesus Christ, through whom we have now received reconciliation.

You can hear the story of Christ's Passion on two levels. One is the purely human level. He was an innocent but brave man who fell foul of the forces of the Establishment, and paid the penalty. He annoyed and challenged the religious authorities of his own people. He called their bluff, showed them up before the ordinary folk. They responded as best they knew how – by blackmailing the Roman Governor into disposing of him, getting rid of him, crucifying him. A story, then, about power, and the misuse of it. We're quite at home with the story told on this level – not exactly comfortable with it, because it is a tale of corruption and cruel cynicism on a large scale: but still, we find it all only too familiar, easy to understand.

There is, however, another level which is infinitely more important. It is the level of Christian belief. Here there is another scene, underlying the first. Here the initiative shifts dramatically. We see Christ sacrificing himself, giving himself up for our sake. In this scene, Annas and Caiaphas and Pilate are unimportant; they could have been any other set of interlocking authorities, in any other century. What matters is *why* this heroic self-sacrifice was necessary. What was *really* going on on Good Friday? So we are going to think about the crucifixion in what you might call a theological way. You may think this takes us a long way from the pain, and the heartbreak, and the tragedy of a very human event. I'll try not to be too technical. After all, we're still dealing with the most loving and caring action in the history of the planet. I certainly don't want to lose sight of that!

From the beginning of time, humankind had carried the burden of its own sin. Conscious, or semi-conscious, of insulting and offending God in so many ways, the human race was impotent to do anything about it. The load of guilt lay upon us like some huge undigested lump; where to put it? What to do with it? How could we ever express to God in an adequate way our regret, our sorrow, our resolution to live henceforth in the light of his face? How could humanity ever unite sufficiently to speak with one voice about all this? It was totally beyond any human capacity. It looked like an alienation which would simply go on and on.

The coming of Jesus is like a watershed: it marks the start of a mended, healed relationship between the human race and God. It is as if God put into *our* hands the means of making the vital gesture which was needed. He allowed the Word, the eternal Son of God, to be human. At last, here was someone with hands and heart free enough to stand before the Father, and by an act more eloquent than any words, express our collective longing. Longing to be forgiven. Longing to be given the means of fighting evil. Longing not to feel separated any more. Longing to be God's intimate family in a way which hadn't been possible since the shadowy, sketchy, mysterious dawn of the Garden of Eden.

I am saying that this gesture of the crucifixion was the appropriate way of atoning for sin. That's a huge thing to say. How could anything so grim be appropriate? Is the Father such a heartless and exacting taskmaster? Or are we rather dealing with what Newman calls, in his hymn, 'O wisest love'? Without the loving, voluntarily accepted death of the cross, there could have been no resurrection. And we needed the resurrection more than anything else in the whole history of the world. The resurrection is for us, literally, a matter of life and death.

Still, the first thought that comes to mind is inevitably this: 'Sin must be a truly appalling thing, to need this kind of recompense. It must be much worse than ever I thought. It can't just be a joke for cracking in pubs, or an old-fashioned myth to be seen as some sort of peasant hang-up. It must be real, and ghastly, and sordid beyond words: because the crucifixion was real, and ghastly, and sordid beyond words.'

This is right. Sin is the greatest of all disasters. To offend God is the ultimate evil. God is the source and inventor of everything that is true or good. To fly in his teeth is to launch yourself into the darkness, like a spacecraft perpetually off-course. John, in his Gospel and in his letters, is almost obsessed with this theme of light and darkness. 'In him was life, and the life was the light of all people. The light shines in the darkness, and the darkness did not overcome it.' 'This is the message we have heard from him and proclaim to you, that God is light and in him is no darkness at all. If we say we have fellowship with him while we walk in darkness, we lie and do not live according to the truth.' John would be the first to tell us: 'Sin isn't only offensive to God, who deserves better of us than that; it is also self-defeating. It is the ultimate choice of nothing.'

Sin comes from inside us. Matthew relates two sayings of Jesus which are very powerful. 'Out of the abundance of the heart,' says Christ, 'the mouth speaks. The good person brings good things out of a good treasure, and the evil person brings evil things out of an evil treasure.' And again, 'Do you not see that whatever goes into the mouth enters the stomach, and goes out into the sewer? But what comes out of the mouth proceeds from the heart, and this is what defiles. For out of the heart come evil intentions, murder, adultery, fornication, theft, false witness, slander.' Three times Jesus uses that word 'heart'. Your heart is, symbolically, the fount of love. It can also be the fount of ill-will. Sin is the conscious choice, the conscious willing of what you know in your heart to be wrong. Here is the fatal ambiguity of humanity – that we are capable of this choice, this willing.

A picturesque description might be this: that I was made to be a unit, a harmonious whole. When my free choice goes on the spree, one way, and my conscience goes the other way, I am split in half. I lose my unity. I lose, in every sense, my integrity. And the splitting of me is a grave affair. After all, the splitting of the atom, deceptively small, has cosmic results. So does sin.

Two things occur to me as a result of all this. One is that we should have the self-confidence to consult our conscience, to listen to our conscience, to take notice of it. It isn't an absurd and truncated piece of outmoded equipment: it is what gives you your dignity as a human being and a child of God. It is the deepest part of you that is accessible. It is what makes you who you are, so treat it with respect!

The other is this: you know that very human trick of pushing things under the carpet? We do this with things that just aren't tolerable. We do it with things we cannot bear to look at. Psychologists have more technical terms to describe it, this operation, but even without professional terminology we know what it is, don't we, from our own experience? I find that sometimes people do this with their sins. Some people are constitutionally incapable of ever saying, 'I was wrong', or, 'It was my fault'! They find this 'shadow' side of their life unbearable to contemplate. I would be like this myself . . . *if* I didn't believe that the crucifixion of Jesus had been a success. But it was a success in this sense, that it achieved what it set out to achieve, which was my forgiveness, and yours. So now I can take the risk of bringing my sinfulness out into the light of day, and looking at it, and not panicking at what I see. It has been allowed for, and atoned for; it is something from which I can recover.

Paul sums it up beautifully in the text from Romans quoted above: 'For if while we were enemies we were reconciled to God through the death of his Son, much more surely, having been reconciled, will we be saved by his life.'

Time for Tenderness

Matthew 27:27-50

Then the soldiers of the governor took Jesus into the governor's headquarters, and they gathered the whole cohort around him. They stripped him and put a scarlet robe on him, and after twisting some thorns into a crown, they put it on his head. They put a reed in his right hand and knelt before him and mocked him, saying, 'Hail, King of the Jews!' They spat on him, and took the reed and struck him on the head. After mocking him, they stripped him of the robe and put his own clothes on him. Then they led him away to crucify him.

As they went out, they came upon a man from Cyrene named Simon; they compelled this man to carry his cross. And when they came to a place called Golgotha (which means Place of a Skull), they offered him wine to drink, mixed with gall; but when he tasted it, he would not drink it. And when they had crucified him, they divided his clothes among themselves by casting lots; then they sat down there and kept watch over him. Over his head they put the charge against him, which read, 'This is Jesus, the King of the Jews'.

Then two bandits were crucified with him, one on his right and one on his left. Those who passed by derided him, shaking their heads and saying, 'You who would destroy the temple and build it in three days, save yourself! If you are the Son of God, come down from the cross.' In the same way the chief priests also, along with the scribes and elders, were mocking him, saying, 'He saved others; he cannot save himself. He is the King of Israel; let him come down from the cross now, and we will believe in him. He trusts in God; let God deliver him now, if he wants to; for he said, "I am God's Son".' The bandits who were crucified with him also taunted him in the same way.

From noon on, darkness came over the whole land until three in the afternoon. And about three o'clock Jesus cried with a loud voice, 'Eli, Eli, lema sabachthani?'; that is, 'My God, my God, why have you forsaken me?' When some of the bystanders heard it, they said, 'This man is calling for Elijah'. At once one of them ran and got a sponge, filled it with sour wine, put it on a stick, and gave it to him to drink. But the others said, 'Wait, let us see whether Elijah will come to save him.' Then Jesus cried again with a loud voice and breathed his last.

There is an hour of the afternoon when it is quite easy to go to sleep. In Latin countries they build this custom into their day. You don't have to be shifty or secretive about it. It's part of life. Everybody's life.

So I was probably being very obstinate one day in August, not long ago. I was attending a conference in a Latin American country. The afternoon was beautifully quiet, and most of my colleagues had wisely retired to their rooms. I decided to take advantage of the peace and the silence, and try to pray a little before the uproar of debate and translation broke out again. I wasn't being pious: just stubbornly different, I suppose.

So I went to the chapel. It was a very simple building, with whitewashed adobe walls and a thatched roof. The roof, I might say, leaked whenever it rained, which was often. But just for the moment it wasn't raining. The earth between the palm trees outside, and in the banana plantations, was steaming in the hot sun, cicadas were whirring away in the bushes, and little lizards were chasing each other up the walls by the altar. There was a torrent of birdsong in the trees.

And suddenly my eyes were riveted on the crucifix which was hanging there on the wall. It wasn't beautiful, graceful, aesthetic, like the kind of carved crucifix you might buy in an Alpine village, or like the exquisite ivory ones the Spaniards used to make. It was plaster, heavy and crude, too big, and painted in primary colours. And what caught my attention most of all were the knees of Christ.

The knees were depicted as cut and bleeding. This makes sense, doesn't it, from what we know? Our Lord had been scourged. He had been forced, in a gravely weakened state, to carry the cross through the streets of Jerusalem and up the hill of execution. The guards who escorted him were anything but gentle. It would be astonishing if he had managed to make this journey without falling, without grazing and bruising his knees.

But I'd never before seen a crucifix which took particular account of the knees of Christ. And this one by some trick of association, made me think of the times I had hurt my knees. Times as a small boy when I was learning to ride a bicycle, but hadn't yet learned how to dismount. Times in the playground when I had tripped and fallen. Times when my leg had come into violent contact with somebody else's football boot.

The remedy was always the same. I searched out my mother, or a teacher, or some other sympathetic adult, and demanded attention. 'Look what's happened.' It was, after all, a fundamental human right to have one's knee inspected, washed and plastered up before it was pronounced usable again. There was a ritual to be gone through with knees. It was often through our knees, wasn't it, that our parents reassured us, 'I still love you; I do care what happens to you'. A lot of human affection, a lot of tenderness, was expressed in the careful sponging, the kissing better, the dabbing with bits of lint and disinfectant. The care was often out of proportion to the injury. In retrospect it might all seem very sentimental. But how important it was. And is.

There is a legend which isn't scriptural, but which is part of the devotional treasury of Catholics, that Jesus' own mother met him on the way to Calvary. She would have been conscious of those knees of his. They would have symbolised for her as nothing else the brutality, the gross cruelty of the whole affair. Because he was going to be crucified, his knees didn't matter any longer. Indeed, his feelings didn't matter either. He'd crossed the invisible line between being a person, deserving consideration, and a thing, to be disposed of. He had crossed it when Pilate had washed his hands and handed him over: remember what Matthew tells us in his Gospel . . . 'They gathered the whole cohort around him. They stripped him and put a scarlet robe on him, and after twisting some thorns into a crown, they put it on his head. They put a reed in his right hand and knelt before him and mocked him.' Feelings didn't matter any more. On the Way of the Cross those physically nearest to him, the mercenary soldiers entrusted with his execution, saw him as a job to be finished before tea, so to speak. Here is a large part of the horror of Good Friday. It's that the time for tenderness is over. And when you say that, you have said the final 'No' to somebody else's humanity.

Maybe because I was in Latin America, and because there were some very poor people just at the end of the drive, my thoughts moved to them, and folk like them. That for many people in the world, too, the time for tenderness is over. They can expect no pity, no reassurance, from anyone. I thought of husbands and fathers picked out of ditches in El Salvador, and whole populations starving on the march in Mozambique, and refugees in wretched camps on the Thai border. How easily we accept that our world is a cruel place. The edge of our indignation is quickly blunted.

It seemed to me then, and it is still my conviction, that the showing of tenderness is very near the heart of what it means to be Christian. And to be part of any system which has renounced tenderness in the name of expediency is the opposite of being Christian. Some people might say that this was absurdly naive; that a certain number of people have to suffer, and that's that. 'But one of them, Caiaphas, who was High Priest that year, said to them, "You know nothing at all! You do not understand that it is better for you to have one man die for the people than to have the whole nation destroyed."' Tired, mature, worldly-wise, John's reporting of the dialogue in the Council has a disturbingly modern ring.

At my conference were priests whose people were being massacred by drug-traffickers, shot as a deterrent to others by government troops, tortured as a matter of course before interrogation in the downtown barracks, thrown off their miserable strips of land to make room for highways and high-tech farms, systematically deprived of all medical help unless they could pay for it.

Once upon a time we could have said, with a sigh that exempted us from all responsibility, 'Well, at least, there's none of that going on here'. It's not so easy today, though. So many of the levers of power, political and economic, do lie in unexpected places. We need a worldly wisdom to match that of Caiaphas, but for a different and opposite purpose. We need it to ensure that wherever our influence spreads, there will be tenderness, there will be regard for the individual, there will be respect for human dignity, no man or woman will be expendable, no person will be treated like a thing.

The same Christ who was crucified is on record, in this same Gospel of Matthew from which the extract above is taken, as saying this: that the kingdom of heaven will go to those who are tender: feeding the hungry and thirsty, caring for the stranger, the sick, the imprisoned. When we say to him, 'Lord, when did we do this?', he will reply, 'Truly I say to you, as you did it to one of the least of these my brethren, you did it to me'.

Suffering Servant
2 Corinthians 1:3-11

Blessed be the God and Father of our Lord Jesus Christ, the Father of mercies and the God of all consolation, who consoles us in all our affliction, so that we may be able to console those who are in any affliction with the consolation with which we ourselves are consoled by God. For just as the sufferings of Christ are abundant for us, so also our consolation is abundant through Christ. If we are being afflicted, it is for your consolation and salvation; if we are being consoled, it is for your consolation, which you experience when you patiently endure the same sufferings that we are also suffering. Our hope for you is unshaken; for we know that as you share in our sufferings, so also you share in our consolation.

We do not want you to be unaware, brothers and sisters, of the affliction we experienced in Asia; for we were so utterly, unbearably crushed that we despaired of life itself. Indeed, we felt that we had received the sentence of death so that we would rely not on ourselves but on God who raises the dead. He who rescued us from so deadly a peril will continue to rescue us; on him we have set our hope that he will rescue us again, as you also join in helping us by your prayers, so that many will give thanks on our behalf for the blessing granted us through the prayers of many.

Suffering of some sort is the lot of every man, every woman. This isn't a morbid reflection, it is an experienced fact. It may be physical suffering – injury or illness; it may be mental suffering – anxiety or depression; it may be spiritual suffering – guilt, or crumbling faith. But suffering of some sort is part of the business of being alive. We don't need anyone to prove that to us. Every one of us carries some kind of a cross: more or less willingly, perhaps determined not to make a fuss about it, saying to ourselves and to others, 'What I have to put up with is absolutely nothing compared with what happens in some parts of the world'. So, not complaining . . . but still suffering.

The reaction of the Christian, when these times of suffering come, is to pray. We may pray a straight prayer of asking: 'Please, God, may this thing go away and leave me in peace.' We may try to resign ourselves to what is unavoidable: 'God, whatever you want is all right by me – but give me more strength, give me some understanding.' We may pray in exasperation a great cry of reproach, like one of the great woman saints of Christian Europe: 'God, if this is how you treat your friends, no wonder you have so few.' But, one way or another, we pray.

And as we pray, we begin to sense that we are treading in someone's footsteps. The trail is already blazed. Someone has been there first, and left some signposts. And that is Christ. Because in his Passion he underwent all those things – physical, mental and spiritual suffering. And in his Passion he prayed all those prayers: 'My Father, if it is possible, let this cup pass from me; yet not what I want but what you want.' 'My God, my God, why have you forsaken me?'

The suffering of Jesus is a great mystery. The intensity of it. The depth of love and obedience which prompted it. The self-emptying it involved. For this was no play-acting, as some twisted forms of early Christianity maintained. Our Lord could not hold part of himself aloof from pain and misery. He was consumed by it, just as we, on a smaller scale, are consumed by ours. Part of the mystery is this, that the Word made flesh could, as Paul said to the Philippians, empty himself, taking the form of a servant. That he could take a human frame, and being human, submit to the annihilation which is, to all appearances, the fate of every human. How could God the Son do this?

Whatever the answer, the *fact* is a great comfort to me. That Christ has pre-suffered my sufferings. He knows, then, the blackness of them, the grimness of them, the sameness and monotony of them, even the progressive horror of them. There is no feeling which is foreign to him, even the sense of being to blame. Remember the scene in front of Pilate's Palace, with the people, the *ordinary* people, who had welcomed him on Palm Sunday, holding him guilty, seeing him as the great betrayer, demanding his death. Not just scribes and Pharisees, but ones he had reckoned as his friends, they blamed him. How would you or I feel at such a moment? We would feel guilty. Paul said to the

Corinthians, 'For our sake he made him to be sin who knew no sin'.

What makes sense of the total sacrifice of the cross? What could reasonably underlie that awful experience, do you think? Surely, the only explanation is Christ's total resolve to crack the problem of human suffering, to roll it back. And he started with the definitive, ultimate, worst of all human sufferings, which is the loss of eternal life. To protect us from that was his prime objective. To do it he had to penetrate evil to its heart. No cosmetic solution would do. Loss of eternal life is perpetual separation from God; for you and me this would be the final disaster, the loss of meaning to our very existence. To rescue us from this, Jesus voluntarily experiences, on the cross, deep separation from his Father. He plumbs the depths of the thing he is saving us from.

There is a legend – only a legend – that when St Peter was in Rome, the persecution by the Emperor Nero got so bad that Peter lost his nerve; he packed up and moved out, leaving the City walls on the south side and taking the road to Naples. He had gone a very short distance when he saw someone coming towards him, and as the figure got closer he realised that it was Jesus. Breathless with astonishment he stopped him, and asked, 'Where are you going, Lord?' and Jesus looked at him and said, 'I'm going to Rome, to be crucified again'. Which, as you may guess, shamed Peter into turning back himself, and facing the persecution with new courage. They built a church there to mark the spot. The church is a reminder of something far more important than the legend. The fact that sometimes, in our flight from suffering, we meet Jesus going the other way – right into the heart of our suffering in order to save us from it.

So suffering, which in my own experience is sordid, non-productive, a complete waste, begins to take on a new light. Christ links it to love. He shows me how it can express love and create good where previously there was none. I know there is an awful danger of sounding glib about suffering, producing packaged solutions to other people's problems, smug little stereotyped words of comfort which give no comfort at all. And I really don't mean to do that. But as a Christian I still want to say this: I know that even my suffering can be redemptive. Isaiah describes it when he talks about the Suffering Servant who was to come. 'When he makes himself an offering for sin, he shall see the fruit of the travail of his soul.' Christ puts a value on my suffering too: he has raised it up, joined it on to his, given it a saving power for my poor world. 'In my flesh,' again Paul, this time to the Colossians, 'I am completing what is lacking in Christ's afflictions for the sake of his Body, that is, the Church.'

All right: it is easy enough to talk about suffering when you are not suffering: easy to philosophise about it. At the time, it is hell. Noble thoughts are hard to have. But when I cry out to Christ, risen from the dead, enthroned at his Father's right hand and beyond the reach of suffering, I am nevertheless calling on someone who is marked by what he has been through. Marked physically, perhaps, by the nails and the spear; but, more important, marked personally. The recollection of Gethsemane, of the approach of Judas, of that series of trials, of the final dread-filled confrontation with the crowd, is still on him. The experience of the scourging and the crowning with thorns and the Way of the Cross has not been blotted out, annulled, by the resurrection. He remembers being crucified, and what it was like, with the thieves on either side. So that I am talking to one who can enter into *my* sufferings, small by comparison to his, but still maximum-endurable for me, maybe more than maximum. He knows what it's like. I do not have to spell it out.

Paul wrote his letter to the Corinthians, part of which is given above, as a seasoned sufferer. It is hard to think of a pain, physical, mental, nervous, which he hadn't undergone. He lived under constant threat. He was aware of a large number of ingenious enemies out there on the edge of his life. Paranoia would have been easy for Paul: to see plots and risks and dangers everywhere. Each day, quite objectively, could turn out badly, with stoning or arrest or imprisonment. To be a travelling preacher of the Gospel, back in the first century, was perilous in the extreme. He was scorched, frozen, worn out, let down, disappointed, locked up, beaten, shipwrecked, and eventually executed. And yet he could talk about 'the God of all consolation, who consoles us in all our affliction'. And he could say, 'As the sufferings of Christ are abundant for us, so also our consolation is abundant through Christ'. He talks about one of the real low-points of his life, on one of his journeys through Turkey; and he realises now that the sheer hopelessness of it all was to make him rely not on himself, but on God who raises the dead.

Here, I suspect, is the heart of the matter. Our education teaches us to be self-reliant, to be in charge, to be in control of our lives. How deprived we feel if, say, we are sent to hospital! It isn't just that our strength seems to have evaporated. It's also being at the mercy of other people, however well-intentioned, however skilled. It's letting other people make decisions for us. And being told only what is good for us to know, and no more – that sort of thing. Trusting is hard. Surrendering yourself to a process governed by others is agony. It is not in our nature.

And this is the nerve God touches in our suffering. 'Trust me', he says. 'Against all appearances, and against all the odds. Trust me. Unless you become like little children you cannot enter the kingdom of heaven.'

And the most notable thing about little children is that they trust their parents. They haven't yet learned to distrust.

Every moment of distress, every hard experience, contains a direct invitation from the Father to trust him. And if, quite out of character, we accept his invitation, and surrender ourselves to him, we find to our astonishment that we are not alone. In the heart of our suffering we find Jesus Christ, and he enables us to say, with him, 'Father, into your hands I commend my spirit'.

Good News to the Poor
Luke 11:37-54

While he was speaking, a Pharisee invited him to dine with him; so he went in and took his place at the table. The Pharisee was amazed to see that he did not first wash before dinner. Then the Lord said to him, 'Now you Pharisees clean the outside of the cup and of the dish, but inside you are full of greed and wickedness. You fools! Did not the one who made the outside make the inside also? So give for alms those things that are within; and see, everything will be clean for you.

'But woe to you Pharisees! For you tithe mint and rue and herbs of all kinds, and neglect justice and the love of God; it is these you ought to have practised, without neglecting the others. Woe to you Pharisees! For you love to have the seat of honour in the synagogues and to be greeted with respect in the marketplaces. Woe to you! For you are like unmarked graves, and people walk over them without realising it.'

One of the lawyers answered him, 'Teacher, when you say these things you insult us too'. And he said, 'Woe also to you lawyers! For you load people with burdens hard to bear, and you yourselves do not lift a finger to ease them. Woe to you! For you build the tombs of the prophets whom your ancestors killed. So you are witnesses and approve of the deeds of your ancestors; for they killed them, and you build their tombs. Therefore also the Wisdom of God said, "I will send them prophets and apostles, some of whom they will kill and persecute", so that this generation may be charged with the blood of all the prophets shed since the foundation of the world, from the blood of Abel to the blood of Zechariah, who perished between the altar and the sanctuary. Yes, I tell you, it will be charged against this generation. Woe to you lawyers! For you have taken away the key of knowledge; you did not enter yourselves, and you hindered those who were entering.'

When he went outside, the scribes and the Pharisees began to be very hostile toward him, and to cross-examine him about many things, lying in wait for him, to catch him in something he might say.

Christ, says Paul, is the first-born from the dead; the first of many brothers. He is the leader of the whole of humanity, and the property of us all: we call him 'Our Lord', and that's correct.

So it is that you will find black ebony statues of Jesus, and pictures of Japanese babies in the stable at Bethlehem. There's a blond British Jesus in stained glass at Ely; and in one cathedral high in the Andes, an oil-painting of a perfect Amerindian Holy Family in the house at Nazareth. It is right that it should be so. No race has a monopoly of Jesus. Christ is no one's exclusive property.

But having said that, we have also to say that God did become man at a particular moment in history, in a particular place, as a member of an identifiable society. He could have done it otherwise, but this was the way he chose. He chose to belong to a subject race. He chose to be a man who worked with his hands, not a professional. He chose to have roots in the distant provinces, not the capital. See how the picture builds up. He chose very humble friends and companions.

It would be fair to say that Jesus was a poor man. Not in the sense of being destitute – there is no evidence for that – but in the sense of being powerless: one of the 'anawim', the great ruck of the Hebrew population, little ones, the ordinary folk. Being without pull, without influence, without recourse, without any say in how your life will develop, or the terms of your employment – these things are real poverty. Now of course it is wrong to read the social attitudes of twentieth-century Western Europe into first-century Palestine. People did not feel the same grievances that we feel, and their perception of justice was different. But, allowing for that, Jesus was still a poor man: one of the anonymous thousands who were without clout and without consequence.

The poor were ripe for manipulation by the learned. Listen to how Jesus describes it. 'Woe also to you lawyers! For you load people with burdens hard to bear, and you yourselves do not lift a finger to ease them.' (Luke 11:46) It is clear from the Gospels that the scribes, the Pharisees, the High Priests, Pilate and Herod all looked down on the poor for different reasons. Because they were unclean, bad observers of the Law; because they were prone to revolt and had to be kept quiet; because they were so easily exploited. 'They devour widows' houses, and for the sake of appearance say long prayers. They will receive the greater condemnation.' (Luke 20:47) So there is grievance there, isn't there? Our Lord sides consistently with the defenceless against the fast talkers and the smooth operators.

Jesus had power, but it was power that sprang from his integrity. He wasn't clergy, so to speak; he had no qualifications, no human mandate. Yet, 'No one ever spoke as this man speaks', and the crowds listened to him and followed him 'because he spoke with authority'.

The harshest words in the Gospel are reserved for the articulate, the controllers of society. 'Whitened sepulchres' he calls the scribes in Matthew's Gospel; 'Go and tell Herod, that fox . . .'; and to Pilate, when Jesus is on trial for his life, 'You would have no power over me unless it had been given you from above'.

With his disciples he is quite uncompromising when it comes to power. At the Last Supper, when a dispute arose among them, which of them was to be regarded as the greatest, he says to them, 'You know that among the Gentiles those whom they recognise as their rulers lord it over them, and their great ones are tyrants over them. But it is not so among you; but whoever wishes to become great among you must be your servant, and whoever wishes to be first among you must be slave of all.' And to the mother of James and John, who attempted some insider-dealing on behalf of her sons, 'Places on my right and my left are not mine to give' – as if to say, 'This is a subject which bores me, because it isn't relevant'. It wasn't relevant because, as he was to say to Pilate, 'My kingdom is not from this world. If my kingdom were from this world, my followers would be fighting to keep me from being handed over to the Jews. But, as it is, my kingdom is not from here.' Jostling for position makes no sense, if there is no earthly rule in prospect: and for Jesus, there simply never was.

And once you begin to think along these lines, other things come to mind. Like, for example, the temptations in the desert. Early in his public life, our Lord is offered a short cut to success: all the kingdoms of the world, with the authority and glory to go with them. A good springboard, you would say, for preaching the Gospel. But no: this isn't the way it is to be, for our Lord has come to

Good News to the Poor 51

preach the Good News to the poor, and he has set his sights on the captives, the blind, the oppressed, and you can't help these from a great height; only from their own level can you speak to them.

When the Pharisees and the High Priests decided that he should be eliminated, it was as a poor man that they targeted and victimised him. He had no powerful friends to speak for him, and his disciples were easily intimidated. He was vulnerable to the classic forms of persecution. They put agents on the fringes of the crowds he addressed, who made notes of the things he said, reported him to the authorities, compiled a dossier on him, jotting down incriminating words and phrases; so that when the time came for his trial, they could say, 'This man said . . .'. When they handed him over to Pilate, it was really on the grounds that he was a public nuisance: 'He stirs up the people, stops them paying taxes, entitles himself king.' All these are ways in which, through the ages, poor people have been nailed and enmeshed. And yet the irony of it was that if Jesus had been willing to aspire to earthly power, the Jewish people would have supported him in his bid. They could not conceive of a Messiah without nationalistic power; the refusal to accept this was Christ's death warrant.

It was as a poor man that our Lord was executed. He was humiliated and treated like a slave. He was crucified partly as a warning to others: 'This is what happens if you fail to stay in line, if you buck the system.' And the psalm he quoted with his dying breath contains this act of faith: 'The Lord has never despised nor scorned the poverty of the poor. From him he has not hidden his face, but he heard the poor man when he cried.'

I believe that the great division in today's world is not between East and West, but between the powerful and the powerless. And as I read the Gospel I see Jesus unmistakably ranging himself on the side of the powerless. He does this both in his life and in his death. It is not that he was preaching anarchy or trying to destroy authority, civil or religious; on the contrary, 'Render to Caesar the things that are Caesar's', and, 'The scribes occupy the seat of Moses, so you must do what they say'. It was simply that he judged those in power very strictly, applied stern principles of fairness to them. The softest spot in his heart was reserved for the beggars, the lepers, the sinners and the no-hopers; and for the thief on the cross at his side he has the most beautiful promise in the whole of Scripture: 'This day you will be with me in paradise.'

There are two lessons here for our world. The first is that if we are deeply committed to Christ, naked ambition is beside the point, because worldly distinction is an illusion. In terms of eternity, it doesn't count. It will be good, then, if we can – even if it falls to us to accept office, and serve the public – remain aloof and detached from the honour it brings. This demands of us a radical conversion, one which, it must be admitted, the Christian world as a whole has never yet managed to make.

The second is this: that there are millions of helpless people in our world. They correspond to the widows and the orphans, the lepers and the blind beggars, the Samaritans and the publicans of Jesus' time. These people are precious to God; woe betide us if through our agency or lack of interest they are ill-treated or victimised. Christ never preached material equality. But he did preach justice. And in our planet today there is a lot of injustice. You and I must work out for ourselves just where we fit into this kaleidoscope of power and powerlessness, of influence and helplessness. We should look at our world with the critical eye of Christ, for only his eye is sure and accurate.

Awake, Sleeper

Romans 8:28-39

We know that all things work together for good for those who love God, who are called according to his purpose. For those whom he foreknew he also predestined to be conformed to the image of his Son, in order that he might be the firstborn within a large family. And those whom he predestined he also called; and those whom he called he also justified; and those whom he justified he also glorified.

What then are we to say about these things? If God is for us, who is against us? He who did not withhold his own Son, but gave him up for all of us, will he not with him also give us everything else? Who will bring any charge against God's elect? It is God who justifies. Who is to condemn? It is Christ Jesus, who died, yes, who was raised, who is at the right hand of God, who indeed intercedes for us. Who will separate us from the love of Christ? Will hardship, or distress, or persecution, or famine, or nakedness, or peril, or sword? As it is written, 'For your sake we are being killed all day long; we are accounted as sheep to be slaughtered'.

No, in all these things we are more than conquerors

through him who loved us. For I am convinced that neither death, nor life, nor angels, nor rulers, nor things present, nor things to come, nor powers, nor height, nor depth, nor anything else in all creation, will be able to separate us from the love of God in Christ Jesus our Lord.

When Jesus was dying on the cross, the centurion pierced his side with a spear and, John tells us, water and blood flowed out. With this detail, John is reminding us of something hugely important. The water of *baptism* gets its power from the crucifixion. So does the *Blood of Christ* received in the Eucharist. The life of Christians today is thus intimately linked to the sacrifice of Christ on the cross.

And when John says that our Lord bowed his head and gave up his spirit, he is saying two things. One – simply, that our Lord died. But also that from the cross he sent his Holy Spirit into the world. The Spirit who lives in our hearts. The Spirit who enables us to believe. The Spirit who triggers off prayer in us, who prays inside us. The Spirit who is the soul and the life of Christians, and of the whole Church – he was breathed forth from the cross. That's what John is saying: *the cross gives life.*

John writes about the crucifixion, but he already knows about the resurrection when he writes. And he knows the effect the resurrection will have on the followers of Jesus. Baptism and the Eucharist will unite them to the risen Christ. As he writes, these things are already happening, all around him.

Yes, for all of us, but more consciously for those of us who belong, in whatever way, to the Church, the resurrection is a continuing experience. When I am baptised into God's family, I experience the resurrection. When I am fed and forgiven by God, I experience the resurrection. When the word of Scripture finds a home in me, and inspires me, I experience the resurrection. It is going on all the time. The resurrection is ours. Why? Because, as Paul says in the passage from Romans quoted above, we are conformed to the image of Jesus. He is our elder brother. Where he goes, we follow.

So all the priorities of the pagan world are stood on their head. Things which previously looked so frightening – tribulation, distress, persecution, famine, nakedness, peril, sword, death itself – all these things are paper tigers. Because Jesus Christ takes us by the hand, as his younger brothers and sisters, and says, 'Stay close to me, and I will take you through all this, and bring you safely out the other side. Because I've been there, and I know the way.' In all these things, then, we are more than conquerors. Nothing to fear.

When, as a priest, I have to officiate at a funeral, I can still be profoundly moved. Even after thirty years, I am not proof against emotion. Especially if it is the funeral of a child, or of someone badly needed by their family and desperately missed; or of the victim of a sudden, tragic death. And yet, with the sadness, there goes a deep conviction. I know that there is something so noble and so deep about the human spirit that it cannot be disposed of at a graveside or in a crematorium. You can't snuff out a human consciousness, a human intelligence, just like that.

That's a pretty unformed hunch, you might say: just a gut-feeling. In fact it is the resurrection of Christ which gives shape to this feeling. It is fascinating to listen to the words of people much nearer to the Easter experience than we are: some of our forefathers in faith. Leo the Great, for instance, writing in the fifth century: 'By dying, Christ submitted to the laws of the underworld, but by rising again he destroyed their power; and so he broke the uninterrupted sequence of death and made temporary what was eternal.'

'Made temporary what was eternal.' Do I really mean that? Do I really mean that a funeral, which looks so permanent and final, is only a temporary arrangement? Yes, that is exactly what I do mean. 'I am the resurrection and the life', says Jesus. 'Those who believe in me, even though they die, will live, and everyone who lives and believes in me, will never die.'

Our Christian ancestors caught and relayed the full power of this fundamental Christian teaching. Listen to Augustine, writing just before Leo: 'Who can doubt that he will give the saints (that's us) his life, since he has already given them his death? Why is human weakness slow to believe that men will one day live with God?' And another preacher, an anonymous one, puts these words into the mouth of Christ: 'I command you, awake, sleeper. I have not made you to be held a prisoner in the underworld. Arise from the dead: I am the life of the dead. Arise, O Man, work of my hands, arise, you who were fashioned in my image. Rise, let us go hence; for you in me and I in you, together we are one undivided person.'

What a totally liberating thing this is: to know that the tide of life is stronger than the tide of death, because by the cross and resurrection of Christ, God has turned the tide.

In the Gospel account he turns the tide with faultless timing. The resurrection does not become apparent immediately after the death of Jesus. God leaves time for the dust to settle. The body is buried, and the sabbath comes. The sabbath gives time to the High Priests and the scribes to breathe a sigh of relief: their major irritant and threat is gone for good. It gives time to Pilate to congratulate himself on having done the only politically possible thing, and having avoided an uprising with very little bloodshed. It gives time to the apostles to bite on the hard bullet of despair, and wonder how to refashion their shattered lives. It gives time to the other disciples of Jesus, like the ones he would meet on the road to Emmaus, to share their overwhelming disappointment: 'We had thought he was the one who would save Israel.' It gives time to all these people to come regretfully or otherwise to this conclusion: as far as Jesus was concerned, Calvary was the last word. Finis, the end.

Then, and only then, does God prove them all wrong. In the dawning of Easter Sunday comes the dawning realisation. It spreads like the ripples on a pond. He is alive. Why look among the dead for one who is alive? He has appeared to Simon. He has appeared to the eleven apostles. He is again a power to be reckoned with, but this time indestructible.

And Paul, in his letters, doesn't stop with the resurrection. Writing to the Romans he assures them of the *continuing* care of our Lord for them, and for all his people. Christ was raised from the dead, and now he is at the right hand of God, interceding for us. A startling thought: that the Son of God holds my interests, my welfare, my eternal destiny, close to his heart, and intercedes for me.

Looking back he can see me far, far behind him on the trail – an indifferent disciple, only intermittently faithful, easily tempted off course by the siren voices of my world – but still his brother; and therefore beloved. Neither death, nor life, nor angels, nor principalities, nor things present, nor things to come, nor powers, nor height, nor depth, nor anything else in all creation, will break that bond.